P9-DTI-057

Preface

I have always derived great joy and satisfaction from seeing a particular place for the first time. I can recall the thrill as a child of riding my bicycle on Saturday mornings through the New England countryside. Those winding Connecticut roads would take me to places that were intensely fascinating to a ten year old. Whether it was a country fair where I could buy homemade brownies for a nickel, or a huge old estate shadowed by ancient oaks and elms, my anxiety to visit new places was quite difficult to manage. I could barely wait to see what would appear around the next curve.

I suppose those early adventures on the bicycle had a dramatic influence on my life as it stands today, for that curiosity is still there and just as intense as ever. It compels me to get into my Bronco and drive until I am too tired to continue. I love to drive just to be able to see a new lay of the land or a different view of the mountain. I love to hike just to reach that plateau beyond the ridge ahead. Unfortunately I cannot go home until I have seen the end of the road or have come to where the trail disappears. Yet even then I can't help but wonder what's around the corner or beyond that stand of aspen.

I suppose the real joy that I experience is not in satisfying my curiosity but in seeing and feeling that new place. I have always had a strong interest in the geology of the land, both in the nature of its origin and the structure of its topography. The diastrophism of our earth's crust has produced an incredible assortment of geologic formations, be it mountains and oceans, or lateral moraines and high alpine lakes. And where there is land there is usually life, and it is often this partnership that creates the personality of a place and cultivates its mystique.

Beyond the experience of feeling these places is the recognition of and appreciation for the utter beauty manifested by them. The zigs and zags of the creek through the valley, the columbine stacked between larkspur and paintbrush, or the alternating bands of red scrub oak and yellow aspen high on a ridge all exemplify nature's symmetrical plan. Here for me is the ultimate thrill; the thrill of discovering these plans and recording them on film. Like treasure hunts at a children's birthday party, the satisfaction of finding the cache, of finding that pastoral scene you never knew existed motivates me to do what I do.

My first visit to Colorado at the age of twelve planted the seed for what later became the desire to live there. Somehow I knew there would be no shortage of valleys to explore and places to feel. My journey began in 1973 with a rented camera and a used Toyota far off in the Wet Mountain Valley. On foot most of the time, I delighted in exploring the endless valleys of the Sangre de Cristo Range. The Toyota took me high atop Engineer Pass in the San Juan Mountains and later led me into the valleys and mesas of the Telluride area. The acquisition of a four wheel drive vehicle took me up into the valleys of the South Platte's origin and over Mosquito Pass to the town of Leadville. It led me to pastoral valleys sustained by meandering creeks. It led me to Brush Creek and Pleasant Valley. In 90,000 miles it took me past Crested Butte over Kebler and Schofield Passes, and on past Aspen to Wolcott, McCoy, and Oak Creek. I visited countless places in the White River National Forest and an equal number in the San Luis Valley. Yet the journey is not over. The places in Colorado that I have not seen far out number those that I have, and I don't think I'll stop until I've seen them all.

I hope that this collection of images reveals some of the places in Colorado that you may not have seen. The "hidden" valleys are not at all inaccessible and can usually be reached by ordinary two wheel drive vehicles; but they are off the beaten track and not to be seen unless you are specifically looking for them. There are countless more valleys to be visited and enjoyed beyond those in this journey, but these particular few seem very special to me.

The images depict places, but are intended to reveal much more. Just as the geology of our earth is dynamic in nature, so is the personality of a valley, river, or mountainside. Time of day, weather, and time of year have a dramatic affect upon the character of these places, and in a visual sense the possibilities for the Colorado photographer are infinite. The change in the personality of a particular scene from morning to evening, or from spring to fall is very broad, and I hope this becomes apparent within the covers of this book.

As the pace of industrial and resort development quickens in Colorado, more and more of the isolated land revealed on this journey may be consumed. I hope that wisdom will be used to plan this development, and that the beauty of the scenes within this book might serve to spread that wisdom.

John Fielder

With the stroke of an artist, Spring paints the June foliage of an aspen forest below Grand Mesa.

The Wet Mountain Valley

My first extended visit to Colorado was during the summer of 1967 at the age of sixteen. Through arrangements made by my uncle, I was hired as a ranch hand on a 400 acre farm in a very unique place. The uniqueness of this place did not fully strike me until years later after I had had the opportunity to see the rest of the state. In fact, trips throughout the western United States did nothing to lessen my feeling for just how special this place really was.

The place that I am referring to is the Wet Mountain Valley. It is situated between the Wet Mountains on the east and the northern one-third of the Sangre de Cristo Mountains on the west. It is unique because of its utter beauty. The Sangre de Cristo Range contains dozens of peaks stretching above 13,000 feet in height, and many that go beyond 14,000 feet. With the valley floor lying at 7800 feet, one can imagine the sensation created by looking up at these mountains from below. A thrill, that for me has not abated in intensity during over 100 trips to the valley, occurs when I descend into it. The access road from the east, State Highway # 69, crosses over the Wet Mountains at about 10,000 feet and proceeds due west towards the town of Westcliffe in the center of the valley. As if the entire range were being hydraulicly lifted into the sky, the Sangre de Cristo's rise and rise, and continue to rise upward until you can hardly believe the height they attain. This particular procession into the valley is extremely dramatic.

The valley is very lush in some places and almost arid in others. Tremendous amounts of water flow out of the Sangre de Cristo's into the valley's creeks and ditches but much of it goes deep into the ground beneath the alluvial deltas of the foothills. Only in the worst of years is there a shortage of water for the valley's farms and ranches. The eastern slope of the range is not precipitous and the gradual descent of the snowmelt has allowed vast forests of aspen and conifers to take hold. From spring to fall to spring again, the Sangre de Cristo Mountains create vistas the likes of which I have seen nowhere else.

The Sangre de Cristo Range is the longest, straightest, and highest continuous mountain range on our planet. When viewed from the east, this linear pattern allows peaks to be seen far to the north and far to the south, with no conceivable end in sight either way. Just as spectacular is the view from atop any of the higher mountains. An endless succession of ridges, valleys, and peaks extends both north and south. There is no other sight like it. From the backbone of the range extend (like the ribs of a skeleton) steep ridges that disappear into the valley floor. Between each of these ridges flow creeks and streams from the highest snowfields to the valley below. Most of these creeks originate at high glacial lakes, or tarns. In fact, there are over 100 lakes and half that number of draining streams that one can explore. Each valley is different and a visit to one is unlike a visit to any other. Some of these valleys have parallel trails, some do not, but access to all is provided by the Rainbow Trail. This trail is maintained by the Forest Service, and at 9000 feet it winds in and out of the drainages up and down the range. It would certainly take years for anyone to visit on foot all of the places that lie hidden within the high

Indian paintbrush hide from the morning sun. This drama unfolds along Sand Creek high in the Sangre de Cristo Range.

valleys of these mountains.

The flora that populate the ridges and drainages of the Sangre de Cristo Range enhance the mystique of the valley. Great stands of aspen carpet the range in patterns that follow the flow of the draining snowmelt. Restricted by altitide, the quaking aspen remain lower in the foothills and provide a contrast in color to spruce, pine, and fir. The conifers go where the aspen do not and survive much better at the higher elevations. The dwarf oak tree, or scrub oak, populates lower ridges and parts of the valley floor. In the valley they will approach ten feet, but rarely make it past six on the higher ridges. During autumn, when the scrub oak are red and the aspen are yellow, glorious scenes appear from one end of the Sangre de Cristo Range to the other. When the valley floor and the high alpine tundra assume their own fall qualities, and when the peaks inherit the first snows of winter, the spirit of this place is revealed.

And delicate fields of wildflowers make their home not only on the valley floor, but high within the alpine tundra. From dandelions and iris in early June, to lupine and columbine in July, the number of varieties is endless. One particular species may grow alone in a small field, or several may mingle to create a pleasing palate of color. There are even special places where a dozen or more varieties may blanket the ground in a dazzling display.

Access to the Wet Mountain Valley is not difficult, but it is certainly off the beaten track and has escaped the discovery of most of the state's residents. Though there are three points of access, no major highways come close to its boundaries. The town of Westcliffe, the seat of Custer County, lies at the junction of these three secondary roads. There are miles of unpaved county roads that allow access to many parts of the valley, the Wet Mountains, and the Sangre de Cristo Range. The valley, itself, is peaceful and sparsely populated. Farms and ranches occupy most of the land, with the production of livestock and grains generating most of the valley's revenues.

Today much remains as evidence of widespread mining activity in the valley one hundred years ago. Most of the old roadbeds are still there; and it is fascinating to explore the remaining buildings and mine structures from that era. From this silver rich eastern side of the Wet Mountain Valley, it is interesting to look across towards the unscarred slopes of the Sangre de Cristo Mountains. A great contrast exists from one side to the other, both in terms of the lay of the land and the purposes for which these two ranges have been used. When the valley was booming the Sangre de Cristo Range was most certainly a haven for all its citizens, a place to retreat when the pressures of living became too great. These mountains were surely a sanctuary for them in their day just as the entire valley is for me today.

Pages 6,7 — The first week in June brings with it the short-lived bloom of the dandelion. Great fields mark the arrival of summer to the Wet Mountain Valley.

A puddle of October rainwater collects falling aspen leaves just above the Huerfano River and just below the Sierra Blanca massif.

Pages 10,11 — *Scrub oak and the quaking aspen protect an old homestead from the approaching winter near Redwing.*

Above: The January sun illuminates crystaline snow in a vain attempt to warm the valley floor.
Right: A look south from Hermit Pass reveals unique topography high atop the Sangre de Cristo Mountains.

*Above: Near Westcliffe, sunflowers
loom high to absorb the rays
of their namesake.*

*Right: Not far away, a 4" thistle
overshadows the rising sun.*

Above: The valley of the Huerfano River sustains as dense a forest of aspen as one will ever see.

Right: A bristlecone pine rises high above Middle Taylor Creek in the Sangre de Cristo Range.

Above: An October view west from Medano Pass reveals a vivid contrast of colors.

Right: Late afternoon light outlines the meandering crest of the Sangre de Cristo Mountains.

18

*Above: Poised to let loose their seed,
thistle wait patiently for early
winter winds.*

*Right: October tundra frames
Horseshoe Lake, a tarn carved by
once great glaciers.*

Pages 22, 23: An evening view west from Hermit Pass ends with the San Juan Mountains. In between lies the great San Luis Valley.

Above: On Medano Pass, above the Great Sand Dunes National Monument, afternoon clouds suggest an evening snow.

Right: Barren scrub oak sketch patterns in frozen snow.

24

Pages 26,27: October aspens enjoy their last week of foliage below Sierra Blanca Peak in the Sangre de Cristo Range.

Above: Early summer and the bloom of wild iris bring joy to the Wet Mountain Valley.

Right: Snowmelt reflects budding aspen trees poised to sprout this year's leaves.

Above: July marks the arrival of Colorado's flower, columbine. This group sit high atop sturdy stems along North Taylor Creek.

Right: A lonely stand of aspen debate the change of season near California Peak.

Above: October's leaves bath along Middle Taylor Creek in the San Isabel National Forest.

Right: The smaller scrub oak possess all of the splendor of their eastern cousins.

Above: Diminutive thistle only enjoy a photographer's recognition low on the valley floor.

Right: Spring runoff in the Sangre de Cristo Mountains nurtures tropical growth.

Above: An October view north from
Medano Pass reveals a scenic
partnership between land and sky.

Right: Sunflowers line the floor of the
Wet Mountain Valley.

Pages 38,39: Man and mountain exist in morning harmony as Horn Peak presides over the valley.

Above: The contrast of conifers and barren aspen is a study in form.

Right: Scrub oak endure a frigid February in the Wet Mountain Valley.

*Above: Sierra Blanca Peak (14,338')
looms high over the valley of the
Huerfano River.*

*Right: A look south from Medano Pass
reveals a peak unwilling to shed its
morning cloak.*

Along The Yampa River

I recall first visiting Pleasant Valley about 1974 with the objective of seeing Colorado's newest ski area and mountain resort. The development was called Stagecoach and I can remember the bustle of construction activity as the resort prepared for its grand opening. A December snow was falling and low lying clouds prevented views of any great distance. I knew I was in a valley through which flowed the Yampa River, but I had no idea just how special a place lay beyond.

My next visit to the area wasn't until several years later when my new objective was an exploration of the headwaters of the Yampa. The Stagecoach resort had apparently gone out of business shortly after it opened, and my curiosity to see what was left took me back into the place I had since found out to be Pleasant Valley. The month was June and the weather clear, and a short drive from the highway revealed a cluster of abandoned condominiums high on the hillside. For many people I suppose the failure of the development was unfortunate, but as I followed the Yampa farther into the valley I began to feel less sympathy for its demise. My journey this beautiful spring day eventually revealed as pastoral a setting as I have seen in Colorado; and it became quite obvious how this little valley had earned its name.

The county road runs east from state highway #131 for several miles, proceeds north for a while, and finally heads west before its rendezvous with Steamboat Springs and highway #131 again. The Yampa River runs beside the road from beginning to end, meandering very deliberately the entire way. From its origin high in the Flat Tops Primitive Area to the entrance to Pleasant Valley, the river is not particularly broad; in fact, it is no more than a creek. However, merging waters from Morrison and Service Creeks draining from the north end of the Gore Range add credibility to its designation as a river. The waters of the Elk River draining south from the Mount Zirkel Wilderness Area increase its size at Steamboat Springs. Later contributions from the snowmelt of the Elkhead Mountains to the north and the Williams Fork Mountains to the south give it the girth it needs to complete its journey to the Green River.

The entire circuitous journey of the Yampa River is unusually scenic, yet there is nothing along the way the likes of Pleasant Valley. Bottom land as fertile and lush as any herd of cattle would ever require borders the creek on both of its sides. From there begins a gradual rise of the land into aspen covered hills. This decoration of the valley walls ends with stately conifers populating the higher mountain ridges. The valley has been formed with perfect symmetry, as both walls rise at similar angles, and the Yampa flows squarely through its middle.

The Yampa River journeys eastward on its way to a rendezvous with Steamboat Springs.

The thrill of visiting this valley, though, is not so much in viewing nature's topographical symmetry, but in witnessing the personality of this place change from one season to the next. Many factors contribute to the dynamic change in the valley's appearance from spring to summer to fall to winter. The metamorphosis is dramatic.

In spring, lime colored leaflets dot aspen trees across the valley walls. Wild grasses by the river and hays in the pastures complement the delicacy of the aspen with their own shades of green. Frost on the fields sparkles in the early sunlight, and clouds of vapor rise above the river through cool morning air. Yellow dandelions and purple wild iris bloom on the valley floor as countless varieties of flora make their spring debut. Shades deepen as early summer storms soak the valley with gentle rains. Colors on ancient rocks change as lowly lichens fasten their skins to outcroppings of stone.

The heat of summer challenges the struggling river; yet only in the dryest of years does the Yampa fail to sustain Pleasant Valley. Still cool waters continue to add color to the valley, and new life is constantly appearing. Scarlet saxifrage and orange poppies take over when iris and dandelions disappear. Though lichens remain the same, the aspen assume new shades of green as they quake in the warm summer breeze. The hays grow taller giving motion to the valley as they sway to the command of an afternoon thundershower. No longer surging over its banks, help from loyal tributaries allows the river to meet the Green miles beyond.

When autumn winds finally arrive, vapor once again rises from the peaceful river. The still slowing Yampa exposes its bed, but to retiring plantlife a shortage of water is harmless now. Autumn is approaching and new colors paint the valley floor. As greens disappear, red, beige, and brown take their predestined places. Stiffening grasses ignore brisk October breezes, and frost returns after a very short absence. Deliberate enough to paint gold next to green, and green behind orange, dense groves of aspen inherit their traditional gold. The October air is thin and still as it awaits the arrival of cold arctic winds. And the flowers are gone, asleep until next year.

The valley prepares to hibernate, for great snows are a tradition in Pleasant Valley. Only tall conifers high on the ridges can resist thick blankets of winter snow. And except for the brittle skeletons of barren aspen trees, all else is covered and forgotten until spring. Even the great river lies buried under snows, wiped off of the valley floor with not a trace left behind. But below thick ice the journey continues for that trickle of water will restart the cycle with the coming of spring.

No longer green and wet,
October ferns assume a new identity
along the Yampa.

46

*Above: Not even dry August denies the
Yampa River valley its due.*

*Right: With their sun behind them,
spring aspen light up the valley floor.*

*Pages 50, 51: Tall summer grasses mix
with crimson saxifrage.*

Above: Pleasant Valley has many moods, but earns its name one calm October afternoon.

Right: The arrival of dusk reveals motionless meanders of the Yampa.

Pages 54,55: In the spring, late rains provide Pleasant Valley a new personality.

Above: Despite the waning snowmelt, the valley remains lush through August.

Right: Along the banks of the Yampa River, groundcover cultivates itself with agrarian discipline.

Pages 58,59: A solitary homestead lays
low in the valley as the Yampa
disappears into the foothills.

Above: September makes her mark on
canyon walls.

Right: Poppies stand tall together to
drink from a small tributary.

In The Vicinity of Telluride

Perhaps because they are so far away is the lure to visit so great, and I probably sleep least on nights preceding planned journeys to Colorado's San Juan Mountains. The assortment of places to explore and scenes to see is so voluminous and so heterogeneous, that I actually become nervously excited preparing to leave. It happens even now and to date I've been to the San Juans dozens of times.

Perhaps because these mountains are so grand do I feel the lure. The number of peaks rising above 13,000 feet in elevation are too numerous to count and those exceeding 14,000 feet are ubiquitous. There are no more staggering views in the entire state than from atop a peak of the San Juan Mountains, and a look in any direction yields a view towards clusters of these same precipitous peaks. In fact, the San Juan Mountains are a collection of several unique mountain ranges thrust together upon one large plateau. From the La Garita Mountains and the Cochetopa Hills on the east, to the San Miguel Mountains and the Sneffels Range on the west, this fusing of separate formations has produced a challenging and spectacularly scenic alpine environment.

Perhaps the interesting and complex history of these mountains provides the lure. From the Tomboy Mine high above Telluride to the boom days of Creede; from the history of Rico, once one of the nation's largest mining camps, to the legend of Alfred Packer, there exists enough history to fill a thousand books. The stories of towns starting with a dream, swelling to urban proportions, and later shrinking to obscurity reoccurs time and again in the San Juan history.

Or perhaps the vast network of old mining roads and renovated jeep trails provides the lure to return. From Creede to Lake City over Slumgullion Pass, from Lake City to Ouray over Engineer Pass, or from Ouray to Telluride over Imogene Pass there exist countless miles of ancient routes through Colorado's most historic territories. With a sturdy vehicle one can drive and bounce over the same roads frequented by mule trains and stage coaches over one hundred years ago. Without ever having to lift a foot, the opportunity exists to climb high peaks or view steep cliffs from the backseat of a Jeep or Scout.

Whatever the lure, these mountains are special and a journey through them is like a journey through no others. And one special portion seems to stand out from the rest, for Telluride enjoys as scenic a setting as any town I have ever seen. Surrounded on three sides by precipitous peaks, sheer cliffs end just on the outskirts of town. In summer spectacular waterfalls cascade to the valley floor, and in winter dangerous snowslides plummet thousands of feet at high rates of speed. Without the path blazed by the San Miguel River, Telluride would be completely hidden by the highest of mountains.

*Larkspur slumber
under the morning gaze of the
Wilson Mountains.*

To the north and east lies the Sneffels Range and the isolated land of the Uncompahgre Primitive Area; and to the south lies the Wilson Mountains Primitive Area. Peaks exceed 14,000 feet in both of these regions, and the Sneffels Range can be seen far to the north from Montrose and Grand Mesa. Its jagged sierra crest gives it a personality enjoyed by no other range; and a particularly scenic vista occurs on Dallas Divide where the view south crosses broad fields of hay and dense groves of cottonwood trees. On the west end of the range Last Dollar Road rambles south to Telluride, crossing high ridges and great mesas offering grazing land to thousands of sheep and cattle.

And it is the mesas that make this southwest corner of the San Juans so special, for nowhere else in Colorado do these broad, rolling plateaus lie so wide below high mountain peaks. Deep Creek Mesa harbors great fields of hay and wild grasses above Telluride, and casually provides magnificent views south to the Wilson Mountains. Small groves of aspen dot the landscape, punctuating the hills with splashes of color. From spring to fall the personality of this mesa changes dramatically as fields of dandelions and budding aspen become beige colored pastures and bright yellow forests. The land is wide open and in any direction there is no end to the path of one's vision.

Just as unique are the mesas of the Dolores River drainage. In between the east and west forks of the Dolores River lie Taylor and Stoner Mesas. High within the San Juan National Forest, these vast plateaus are covered with aspen. Stacked side by side, one behind the other, these masses of trees extend for miles and miles, and I don't think there are aspen forests any broader in Colorado. In spring, blizzards of lime colored leaflets decorate the forks of the Dolores River; and in autumn, variegated tones of green, yellow, and orange mingle with one another up and down the valley walls. And there are definite patterns to the change; as if a painter was shading his picture, the transition from one color to the next is almost always gradual. The result is nothing less than one of nature's finest masterpieces, painted over thousands of acres of lonely mesas and isolated alpine terrain.

This forgotten part of Colorado, forgotten because almost nothing is near, is a joy to visit and to experience. From Dallas Divide to Lizard Head Pass the topography is like no other, and a great opportunity awaits the Colorado photographer. As difficult as it normally is to find those special moments in time, the scenic valleys and mesas around Telluride facilitate the search.

In a state of transition, September's aspen greet a late summer storm along the West Dolores River.

64

*Above: Dandelions texture great fields
on the Wilson Mesa.*

*Right: Soon to become quaking forests,
June's aspen enjoy a very brief stage
between budding and maturation.*

*Above: A falling sun focuses upon Mt.
Sneffels and the Sneffels Range.*

*Right: Tall aspens are not the only
source of autumn color.*

Pages 70, 71: A rising moon appears through aspen trunks above the West Dolores River.

Above: A glacial erratic lays beneath the gaze of Mt. Wilson (14,246').

Right: Rolling fields above Telluride manifest the unique topography of the San Juan Mountains.

Pages 74, 75: The color of immature aspen leaves is spectacular, yet transitory in duration; even more so than their better known fall state.

Above: Last Dollar Road, between Dallas Divide and Telluride, is an avenue of spectacular vistas.

Right: Looking south from Last Dollar Road towards the Wilson Mountains.

Above: The Sneffels Range fends Telluride on the north. The historic town is sheltered on three sides by tremendous peaks.

Right: Looking west, Ouray lays below and Telluride not far beyond.

Above: A herdsman takes his sheep down from the high country and home for the winter.

Right: A setting sun isolates two aspen and saturates them with light.

Above: Tremendous forests of aspen populate the banks of the West Dolores River.

Right: Scrub oak and aspen coordinate their colors below Mt. Sneffels .

Above: Leafing aspen along Last Dollar Road create a blizzard of leaflets.

Right: Lizard Head rises high in the distance as summer returns to the San Juans.

*Pages 86, 87: Mt. Sneffels
dominates a mid-September scene.
Telluride
lays beyond and below.*

*Above: Spruce and scrub oak find
room to survive amidst the dense
forests of the Dolores River drainage.*

*Right: The morning sun illuminates
spring's aspen.*

Pages 90, 91: A sheepherders refuge
emerges from winter ready for
another summer's occupation.

Above: Autumn arrives below the
north face of Mt. Sneffels.

Right: A weather-worn barn
makes a contribution to nature's
autumn scene.

Above: The light from the sun constantly finds ways to highlight the symmetry of the land.

Right: A clear June afternoon yields a view of Lizard Head (13,113'), an ancient volcanic neck.

*Above: The lay of the land reveals
nature's own symmetry.*

*Right: The forests of the San
Miguel Range pave a forgotten road.*

Headwaters of The South Platte's Middle Fork

Just a few years ago I discovered a place that could be reached in a relatively short period of time, with unique and exciting topography and very easy access. Like the San Juan Mountains, its history originated in the mining camps and its hills are riddled with century old roads. Its peaks often exceed 14,000 feet and the high glacial valleys form the headwaters of a very significant drainage. It is an immensely scenic area with a complicated geology and a great representation of alpine life, and it produces vistas in all directions that delight the eye.

The place is the Mosquito Range and the drainage is the Middle Fork of the South Platte River. Located in the central Rockies of Colorado, it begins at Hoosier Pass and ends only thirty miles later northeast of Buena Vista at Trout Creek Pass. Its northern end is populated with the likes of Mt. Lincoln (14,284'), Mt. Democrat (14,142'), Mt. Cameron (14,238') and Mt. Bross (14,110') whose well protected snowfields insure ample runoff to the South Platte River. With contributions from Mosquito Creek and Buckskin Creek to the south, and support from the South Platte's South Fork draining from the Weston Pass area, the river makes its famous rendezvous with Denver many miles later.

Once the high grade ores began to play out in Leadville, prospectors crossed the Mosquito Range over Mosquito Pass and found their way down to the eastern slope. The discovery of gold in the 1860's produced boom towns the likes of Buckskin Joe, Montgomery, and Mosquito high in the upper valleys of the range. The discovery of silver in the 1880's perpetuated the boom and the Mosquito Pass road became nothing less than a thoroughfare between Leadville and Como. By stage, freighter wagon, by horseback and on foot, fortune seeking men wore well beaten roads into the Mosquito Range.

Though the years of intense mining activity left deep scars upon the land, the scenery is still very special. From atop the range the view across South Park yields a unique portrait of the backside of Pikes Peak. To the west lies Leadville and a magnificent look towards the Sawatch Range and Colorado's highest peak, Mt. Elbert. To the north lie Breckenridge and the craggy peaks of the Ten Mile Range. Within this great watershed, the wildflowers are as prolific and as varied in kind as I have seen anywhere in the state. It is not uncommon to see half a dozen species clustered together on one wet slope, and I recall one place where a dozen or more mingle with one another each year in July. What is particularly interesting is the variety of life above 13,000 feet on the highest of ridges. From the oranges and greens of ubiquitous lichens, to the scarlets and blues of gentian and forget-me-nots, there is enough color on high to fill any roll of film.

For just a quick trip from Denver this place is quite special. Its high glacial valleys provide numerous ways for one to enjoy the alpine environment; be it views of far away ranges or hikes through fields of mountain bluebell, yesteryear's miners have provided access to a magnificent alpine domain.

With Pikes Peak in the distance, the original waters of the South Platte's Middle Fork wind through glaciated valleys.

Above: Winter snows recede around a glacial tarn high in the Mosquito Range.

Right: Autumn tundra catches fire backlit by a falling sun.

Pages 102,103: The burial of summer
grasses begins with an early
November snow.

Above: The remains of summer's color
provide stark contrast to winter's
white snow.

Right: Great varieties of wildflowers
inhabit the glacial valleys of the
Mosquito Range. Gentian, bluebell,
and sandwort are a few.

*Above: "Unpredictable" best describes
high alpine weather. A storm moves
quickly to soak the land.*

*Right: An evening sun peeks through
ancient bristlecone pines.*

Pages 108, 109: Indian paintbrush, larkspur, and columbine blanket the earth below Mosquito Pass.

Above: Afternoon showers threaten the tranquility of the Middle Fork of the South Platte River.

Right: Paintbrush and columbine claim the space left by a conifer long gone.

Above: Mountain bluebell make a home amidst rugged talus high in the Mosquito Range.

Right: Penstemon and bluebell await morning showers along the Continental Divide.

Above: The view west from Mosquito Pass reveals the northern end of the Sawatch Range.

Right: Ubiquitous lichens paint impressions upon the talus just below Mosquito Peak.

*Above: Delicate autumn color paints
the tundra near Alma.*

*Right: The colors of summer
are intense at the 13,000' level
near Mosquito Pass.*

*Pages 118,119: July rains wash away
remaining snow along the
Continental Divide.*

Along Brush Creek

The creation of any scene is dependent upon a combination of elements. The topography of the area, the plantlife that it sustains, the weather and conditions of light shape the personality of a scene. One condition may overshadow the others but every beautiful scene requires the favorable combination of all four. In and out of valleys across Colorado, the element of plantlife often determines the personality of an area; and no single species dominates the denizens of slopes and drainages more dramatically than the quaking aspen tree. Where water goes, so goes the aspen, covering moist ridges and carpeting valley floors as it follows the path of melting snows. Cottonwood trees cluster beside creeks and rivers, and conifers dominate terrain much higher and dryer, but aspen own the territory in between. Spreading their roots to multiply their kind, the fecund aspen grows tall rapidly during its relatively short lifetime. Through its year long cycle of life, the aspen is more dynamic in a visual way than any other tree. From spring to summer and from fall to winter it assumes a new personality with each change of season. From the pale green leaflets of spring to gold plated boughs of autumn, its leaves give this tree its character. Delicate in construction and translucent in nature, each season's leaves react magnificently to light. When lit from behind, the pastels of spring and the darker greens of summer, and the yellows and oranges of autumn create jewels in the sky.

There are certain areas in Colorado where aspen truly dominate a scene, and one of these is the valley through which flows Brush Creek. Originating in the northwestern foothills of the Sawatch Range, its waters weave through miles of pasture before merging with the Eagle River. From Crooked Creek Pass to Red Table Mountain to the old town of Fulford vast forests of aspen line the ridges and hills. From the highest parts of the ridges to the pastured steps above Brush Creek, these stands of tall trees blanket the earth. Where the aspen do not go, the scrub oak do, and the result in fall is an array of colors the likes of a New England autumn. And below mingling aspen boughs lies the wet forest floor. Remains of old forests and sprigs of new life create their own palates of color from one season to the next.

A quiet place well off the beaten track, this pastoral little valley sustains hardy livestock and healthy fields of hay. Other than during the glory days of the century old mining town of Fulford, life here has always been as peaceful as the waters of Brush Creek itself. A visit to this place invites only the use of one's own senses. To sit and view the endless trunks of aspen, or to feel the wind that quakes the leaves, or to touch the wetness of the valley floor is a wise use of one's time along Brush Creek.

A September moon rises above Brush Creek's valley walls.

*Above: Brush Creek's valley
is fertile territory for great
stands of aspen.*

*Right: Evening sunlight illuminates
tall inhabitants of the valley floor.*

Pages 124, 125: In late September,
scrub oak and aspen lend color to the
spectacular valley.

Above: Brush Creek sustains all life in
the small valley.

Right: With the hand of an artist, the
forest paints its way up and across
the valley walls.

The Others

The mountains and valleys of Colorado special enough to warrant a return trip are countless. Some of these valleys lie high in the ranges protected by great ridges and some lie low in broad basins. Many of the mountains provide unique and far reaching views, others deserve attention just for the life they sustain. Whether on high or down low, whether the view may be for miles or just inches, every mountain and every valley is special. It is merely by the way the eye sees or the camera records that interesting scenes are created and captured. These scenes are everywhere present, and with the aid of nature's own symmetry the ways to delight one's eye are endless. And endless becomes infinite when the effects of light and weather are considered with the other factors. Any and every scene manifests beauty if the perception of the beholder is only barely acute.

In the Ragged Mountain area, broad fields of aspen populate the flat mesas along Kebler Pass. Spring and fall are particularly rewarding times to visit the great forests penetrated by this scenic pass. Running from Crested Butte to the Paonia area, the road does not reach the high elevations, but does pass over spectacular topography. Parallel to Kebler Pass goes the Schofield Pass road. A much more treacherous route, the basin that it penetrates is spectacular not for its aspen but for the conifers lining its high ridges. And draining south from the West Elk Mountains, Ohio Creek meanders quietly through lush pastures towards a rendezvous with the Gunnison River.

Lonely plains sustaining the towns of McCoy, Toponas, and Oak Creek stretch from the Flat Tops to the Gore Range, yet within the monotony of their flatness lie scenes just waiting for a perspicacious eye. Beyond to North Park where broad plains are surrounded by towering mountains, the eye need not be so sharp. And a few very unusual places need little help from the quality of light and the characteristics of weather to make their beauty plainly apparent. The high valleys on both sides of Independence Pass, where meandering creeks wander through fields of tundra, are but two.

And if you were curious to know just what lies beyond the Sangre de Cristo Mountains, if you were anxious to discover if that same extraordinary scenery repeated itself just over the crest, then you might be pleasantly surprised by what lies in the San Luis Valley. Your eye must be perceptive, for its most extraordinary scenes can be illusive; but there is no limit to either delighting one's eye or in just feeling the joy of being there.

Like the patches of snow, spruce trees dot the valley floor below Cinnamon Pass.

*Above: October's aspen reflect
in a beaver pond along Kebler Pass
near Crested Butte.*

*Right: Autumn traditionally arrives
early below Independence Pass.*

Above: A rising sun backlights aspen around Kebler Pass.

Right: Young cottonwoods make their own contribution to the autumn scene.

Pages 134,135: Cottonwood trees line
Medano Creek in the Great Sand
Dunes National Monument.

Above: Marsh grasses sprout from a
beaver's pond near Kebler Pass.

Right: The chill of an
October morning vaporizes waters
of Dillon Reservoir.

Pages 138,139: A new day arrives
in eastern Colorado near Sterling.
The morning light reflects upon the
South Platte River.

Above: The Castles overlook a
productive hay field along Ohio Creek
near Crested Butte.

Right: The White River National Forest
hibernates beneath January snows.

Above: Skiers enjoy fresh powder snow in Sun Down Bowl behind Vail Mountain.

Right: A trio of columbine bask in the sun along Mariposa Creek in the White River National Forest.

Above: Translucent aspen leaves catch fire with help from a rising sun.

Right: Dying flora add color to tundra below the summit of Mt. Evans.

*Pages 146, 147: Rock Creek is a
tributary of the Colorado River.
McCoy awakens to the sound of its
waters and the presence of its
cottonwoods.*

*Above: Tremendous aspen
forests populate the plateau north of
Kebler Pass.*

*Right: Summer approaches near
Ruedi Reservoir in the White River
National Forest.*

Pages 150, 151: The waters of the East
Fork Williams Fork Creek originate in
the Flat Tops Primitive Area. They
provide sustanence to great forests.

Above: Larkspur and iris proliferate
on Grand Mesa.

Right: Dying grasses surround
Summit Lake below Mt. Evans.

Above: Cottonwood trees explode in flame like colors at the Great Sand Dunes National Monument.

Right: Abandoned during the days of drout, an old homestead casts shadows near Brush.

Pages 156, 157: Ohio Creek sustains great fields of hay and pleasant views.

Above: December snowmelt replenishes the frigid waters of the Eagle River near Edwards.

Right: Clouds and aspen imitate the shape of one another near Buford.

Above: Aspen line
a dry creek bed near Wolcott.
There must be water below.

Right: Great sunsets are a
matter of course above the
Front Range near Denver.

Pages 162, 163: Fireweed lines the treacherous Schofield Pass road between Aspen and Crested Butte.

Above: The Rawah Range overlooks cattle grazing the lonely fields of North Park.

Right: Below Independence Pass, the Roaring Fork River begins its journey towards a rendezvous with Aspen.

Above: Nodules of lichen consume a disappearing rock.

Right: Immature aspen color the forest near Oak Creek.

*Above: Barren aspen play games on a
fresh December snow.*

*Right: November snows sketch a frigid
picture near State Bridge.*

Above: Aspen trees await the arrival of spring on Grand Mesa.

Right: Cattails rise high into the sky along the Colorado River.

A skier's solitary tracks wind through conifers of the White River National Forest.

Solitary ski tracks and a falling sun
mark the end of the day somewhere in
the White River National Forest.

About Equipment and Technique

The photographs within this book were taken with three cameras: a large format Wista 4x5 field camera using lenses from 75mm to 300mm, a medium format Pentax 6x7 reflex camera using lenses from 45mm to 200 mm, and a 35mm format Canon F-1 using lenses from 24mm to 200mm. A polarizing filter was used occasionally to increase contrast on the film, and a yellow filter was used in snow scenes to reduce the blue cast on white snow. Most of the exposures for the medium and large format cameras were calculated with a Pentax spotmeter. With all of the cameras, a tripod and cable release were used almost without exception. Kodachrome 25 roll film was used exclusively in the Canon, Ektachrome 64 roll film in the Pentax, and Ektachrome 64 sheet film in the Wista.

In general I think that photographers place too much emphasis upon the brand and type of equipment that they use. There are too many other more important ingredients that contribute to putting a fine image onto film. Factors such as composition, depth of field, exposure, and conditions of light all have a much greater influence than the equipment upon the quality of the photograph. The difference in the optical quality of cameras of the same format becomes insignificant when one considers just how much control he has over the use or misuse of those other factors. The size of the format and the convenience of operating the camera should be a photographer's main consideration in choosing equipment.

For example, as the format increases in size so does the chance of having fine detail in lithographic and photographic reproductions. Yet even with 35mm equipment, the use of a fine grained film, such as Kodachrome 25, will produce extremely sharp images. The stability of the camera, the internal vibrations of its mechanisms, and the conditions of light can also have a dramatic effect upon the resolution of a transparency. Ignorance of these factors can reduce even a 4x5 transparency to mediocrity. And consideration must be given to the convenience of using a camera. Working in the field often requires quick response to the changing condition of one's environment, be it fading light or an approaching storm, and the speed with which one can operate the camera greatly affects productivity.

The efforts of the photographer must be directed towards those factors over which he has the greatest control. He must compose a scene in such a way that the objects within it relate to one another in symmetry. The eye demands this. To aid in composition, he must use the refraction of light within his camera to create the desired depth of field. He must employ the dynamic quality of light to create pleasing combinations of color; and he must be aware of how the scene will expose upon his film and use the contrast of light as a tool to shape the image.

And he must experience nothing less than joy when a fine photograph is the reward for his effort.